MW00463555

take what you need

*a collection of life lessons and
words of encouragement
for people who never settle*

I

Copyright © Abiola Babarinde, 2018

All rights reserved. No part of this publication may be reproduced, distributed, or transmitted in any form or by any means, including photocopying, recording, or other electronic or mechanical methods, without the prior written permission of the author, except in the case of brief quotations embodied in critical reviews and certain other non-commercial uses permitted by copyright law.

For permission requests and other enquiries, please contact the author at _info@abiola.me_.

ISBN 978-1-7286-6883-3 (paperback)

First edition, 2018

To my wonderful friends and family for always encouraging and affirming me.

For everyone who has ever connected with my work. Thank you.

© Abiola Babarinde 2018

may these words make you expectant
for the richness that life has to offer.

INTRODUCTION

Over the past six years, I have been searching.

Exploring, desiring and piecing together the life that I believe I am destined to live. It began with daring to challenge unspoken assumptions about my place in the world, in search of a more fully-formed self. A more authentic self. One who navigates the different phases of life with a confident clarity that outweighs fear.

The challenge with such a significant existential quest is that life gets in the way. Inner demons, external hurts and unpredictable circumstances threaten to exhaust us. This leaves space for doubt to creep in. An internal dialogue begins: *Is it worth it? Was it all in my head? If it's not broken don't fix it, things might not be ideal, but they are good enough.*

When the darkness of difficulty descends, or the busyness of success distracts us, it can be challenging to discern your next step. It becomes all too easy to coast, to sit back and let others dictate your direction. Until you finally lift your head above water, wondering how you ended up in the middle of nowhere.

Even though there is no one and no thing that can give you a step-by-step plan of your life up front, part of our responsibility as humans, and as a community is to remind each other of who we are and why we started this journey in the first place. We owe it to ourselves to encourage each other to keep searching and resist the temptation to take the easy, inconsequential way out.

This is the driving force behind this book. In the following pages you will find a collection of reflections from my life, a life of pursuing purpose and meaning. This is by no means a finished process, but it is the story so far, and it is my gift to you.

My intention is that between these pages, you will find ideas that propel you closer to the person you are destined to be. That you will look again at your life, making conscious decisions about what can stay, and what has run its course. My intention is that as time goes on, you will bookmark and revisit different principles for times when you need them the most. That you will take what you need, exactly when you need it.

I have also included journal pages for you to record your own reflections and responses as you read. In the spirit of our collective journey, please visit our dedicated community page, takingwhatineed.com. Here you will find life lessons shared by other readers and you will be able to submit your own. Thank you for sharing this experience with me. I hope you enjoy reading it, as much as I enjoyed writing it.

— Abiola, 2018

I

mind, soul + self

mind, soul + self

Sometimes the things we cannot see matter the most.

I have learned that despite what society has taught me, these three elements come first: mind, soul and self. For the first five years of my professional life, I prioritised 'doing well' above them all.

It is an easy thing to do because it is easier to focus on what can be quantified, touched and measured. In our attempts to 'do well', we run the fatal risk of neglecting the intangible: true wellbeing. This is what sustains us for the long-run, and I am here for the long-run.

When I faced a crossroads in my career, I shared my frustrations with a brilliant friend. In this discussion I realised:

> *It is not about 'what <u>should</u> I do with my life'. It is about figuring out what will allow my soul to <u>flourish.</u>*

All along I had been focusing on the wrong question, probably because the question of the soul is much more difficult to grasp. You cannot look it up, and no one can tell you what it is. The only way to grapple with this concept is to get really acquainted with the unique landscape of your own soul: what brings peace? What brings energy and what disturbs it? What was it created to do in the first place?

This also required working through joyous and grievous experiences that had been pushed into the corners of my mind, so that I could 'get on with life'. It meant amplifying the quiet whispers of my inner-self and turning down the volume on all the external pressures. Decoding complex thoughts and emotions is a life-long task. But thank goodness, we have our whole lives to figure it out.

Alternatively, you could take the simpler route. The route where we spend our days striving towards an external definition of what it means to 'do well'. A system that involves mindlessly running towards goals set by someone else, hoping that one day it will all make sense. A place where we finally prove that we can rise against the odds, defy the naysayers and finally prove our worth.

But where does 'worth' come from? Do we acquire it by reaching goals, or is it a seed that we are born with, that develops as we develop? Perhaps we are made to nurture and protect this seed.

If we choose the simple route, a tension develops within. At first, our internal needs are quiet. They bend, and they contract as you pour yourself into fulfilling commitments and expectations that were never meant for you.

Eventually, when they are tired of being silenced by demands to have more and do more for everyone but yourself, they stop. They stop stretching and they start screaming: *we are dying.*

And if they are dying, then so is a part of you. And surely that is a price too high for any of us to pay.

When we learn to preserve and protect these three intangibles, we become free. No longer are you pressed into a box, no longer are you exhausted in a way that sleep cannot repair. Finally, you find yourself.

. . .

Never underestimate the power of a mind made up.
Too many of us wait for other people to set the pace.

Growth is not always gentle.

It takes domination. Not by force, but by unapologetically embracing your unique path.

Uncertainty is never sold separately from new adventures.

You cannot control everything.

Simple truths I wish I remembered.

All information is not created equal.

Never hesitate to apply a filter. Test and approve what is allowed to leave an imprint on your mind.

"You don't get what you need because you never ask"

Start asking.

Keep it simple: understated yet understood
by the few who matter.

The people you care about most will eventually see past
an act, because they are desperately looking for *you*.

Authenticity.

Comparison distracts and suffocates.

Breathe.

There are times when the only answers you can find are in the silence.

So take a step back from the voices.
(You know who and what they are.)

Creating brings you closer to who you really are,
especially when you feel like you have lost yourself.

Do the work.

Overextending yourself to save everyone...
but yourself.

Priorities.

Take time to establish values that are consistent with who you *really* are.

Having a stance might bring some opposition, but those who value you will respect it in the long-run.

The weight of exhaustion amplifies anxiety.

Rest.

You can either choose to accept or reject the external narratives placed on you.

Craft your life.

You have a choice.

A choice to shift the narrative.
A choice to change direction.

And no-one has to live with it except you.

There are times when seeking many opinions will only leave you more confused.

Value your inner compass.

Pour yourself a glass of wine,
you will be fine.

taking what I need
space for you to respond + journal your own thoughts:

II

relationships + connection

relationships + connection

The second greatest commandment is to love our neighbour as ourselves. What captures me is the interplay between the two – you cannot love your neighbour if you do not love yourself. And can we really love ourselves, can we *really* value our humanity over our achievements, possessions or appearance, if we refuse to acknowledge the humanity of others? The two are intrinsically linked.

It makes sense that the two are intrinsically linked because each relationship is a type of **connection.** And therefore, the health of *all* of our relationships, with self, with others romantically and platonically somehow connect, like a network of veins and arteries that keep us alive. Because of this connectivity, compartmentalising is a futile task. If you are dealing with mistrust in one relationship, it will show up somehow elsewhere. You cannot fight the overspill.

Managing these connections can get messy because people are messy, including you and me. Who wants to depend on someone who is still dealing with their own baggage? Somehow, in all of this stickiness, there is a sweetness that we cannot live without. We are designed for **interdependence.**

There is also a balance to be struck there are seasons that require solitude. Life, while girded by kindred spirits, is ultimately a pilgrimage that we make alone. **Co-dependence**, the excessive reliance on a person, can be equally problematic. Even though keeping 'someone there' takes the edge off, it prevents us from spending time with the most complex person in our lives, whose secrets we know all too well: ourselves.

If this is you, let this be the beginning of your personal reformation. Examine why you are clinging so tightly to someone else at the expense of yourself. This is your reminder that the harder you cling, the more you haemorrhage life from those healthy veins and arteries in your system. It is time to thoughtfully prune the relationships that no longer work and focus on the ones that need more of your attention.

Those who pride themselves on their **independence,** whose life circumstances have required them to depend on themselves, also have some work to do. Like me. More specifically, we have some barriers to dismantle. Although the journey is yours and yours alone there are companions that make it possible. Your 'defence mechanism' might be starving you of one of the cornerstones of human existence: connection.

Learn to walk in-step with others, collaborating and co-labouring with those who are also trying to make the most of this bewildering but beautiful life.

. . .

The people matter.

"Two are always better than one."

Partnerships are powerful. In the art of love, war and business.

Vulnerability feels like you are putting your life on the line but in reality, you are saving it.

Open up.

When darkness falls, anxiety pushes us towards
isolation.

Yet in order to survive, we *need* to stretch outwards to
the kindred souls that surround us.

Never be afraid to have expectations and set them high. You only get what you ask for.

Forgiveness is not the same as allowing someone to occupy the vulnerable places where they hurt you again.

It is not your job to control every external narrative of your life.

Otherwise, you will spend your existence cleaning up messes you never made.

Healthy relationships bring out the best in you.

If you are always at your worst around specific souls, this is your sign to recalibrate.

Sometimes,
moving on without them
is an act of strength in itself.

The beauty of life is found in the quiet personal places, just as it is found in community and connection.

Why do you bury the rawest parts of yourself to become more palatable to 'friends'?

Can't you see the cement walls you have created?
Can't you see that they have tried to knock them down?

But now, they are *tired*.

Maybe it is easier to connect with people online because it comes with fewer expectations.

True friendship means that you are all in – on days where it is convenient, and days where it is not.

There is intimacy in sharing struggles and successes.

Maybe the point of sharing your faith isn't to tell people 'the answer' or convince them of anything...

Maybe those conversations are simply seeds that bloom when the time is right.

Faith only feels restrictive if you
a) do it to prove yourself and;
b) do it in **isolation.**

Find your family.

Trust issues are not always about the person in front of you.

Sometimes they come from the insecurities of the person in the mirror.

We could all benefit from a bit more grace and compassion.

Second, third and fourth chances matter.
Starting with yourself.

'Times have changed'
but the human condition has not...

Technology has developed, and trends have shifted. But the fundamentals stay the same, so do not be so quick to discard history.

The packaging is just different.

taking what I need
space for you to respond + journal your own thoughts:

III

purpose + the process

purpose + the process

Without fail, the question of Purpose and The Process is always asked by my readers and audience members. Like a resistant strain of bacteria, it seems to be the battle that our generation is fighting collectively. We feverishly gather around with our mouths agape, desperate for answers, hoping that someone will step down from on high and give us the perfect formula for finding purpose.

But there is no formula. All we can do is engage in a process of following the signs that point us towards where we are meant to be. These signs are less clearly defined than we would want, and there is a reason for that. They are not clearly defined because part of our responsibility is to live out our purpose daily. This process draws us to the edge of risk: risking the familiar; risking relationships, or risking our previously imagined version of ourselves. Most importantly, we risk the comforting yet vacant applause of a crowd who are just as clueless as we are.

Someone I admire once quipped 'it is a privilege to think'. Now more than ever, we are living life on demand. We click a button and immediately get an experience, a product or a person delivered to us. In the cacophony of messages that decorate daily life, much of the thinking has already been done for us. The promise of efficiency and outsourcing unimportant tasks has been fulfilled.

The problem is that this behaviour slowly creeps into the more complex areas of our lives: the places that require the heavy lifting of critical thought.

Critical thought involves questioning where the aspirations and expectations that we impose on ourselves really come from. It is true that we cannot escape the influence of each other, but we owe it to ourselves to take the raw materials of what society recommends and craft it into something customised. This is what many of us miss. We happily — and sometimes unknowingly — collect so much from others that our minds are brimming with content, leaving no space to do anything with it all. We have exchanged the profound for the convenient, leaving us craving more depth.

Like a skilled craftsman, our responsibility is to first develop discernment. To seek out the finest raw materials, and discard the cheap imitations that hawkers thrust in our faces for a quick sale (or a quick follow, quick view, quick click). Then, with a faint vision in mind, we start to arrange, shave, cut and craft the raw materials into something more meaningful.

It is easier to be a passive recipient than to turn away the hawkers and wait patiently for higher-quality materials. It is easier to add more to the pile than to commit to the days spent engaging in the laborious process of creating a masterpiece. The irony is that as we engage in this work, the vague vision becomes clearer: it is revealed *in* the process.

I wonder whether we need to stop asking what our purpose is, and start challenging ourselves to grow the courage to act on what we *think it might be*. There is weight in asking yourself the big questions: *what are the right materials for me? What am I willing to substitute and what must stay? That takes courage.*

This is not a single act of courage however, it is a series. A collection of giant leaps and amateur attempts to beat the odds. It can be as small as reviewing that draft one more time, to more radical transitions into a new city, a new job, a new relationship or an entirely new life. The moments when you feel like a novice and moments when you are sought out for your expertise. This is the process of pursuing purpose.

Are we ready for that? Are we prepared for the reality of life? The path of purpose is more prickly than glossy stories that fit neatly into 800-word editorials. If we keep walking, keep engaging in and keep trusting the process long enough, finally, somehow, we make it 'there'.

· · ·

Purpose is revealed in the process.

God guides your *steps* – not just your strategy.
Start today.

Proverbs 16:9

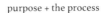

Confirmation comes from going on the journey itself.

You cannot validate your purpose if you have got nothing to work with.

Every experience is an opportunity for the manifestation of different gifts.

Nothing is wasted when your heart is committed to uncovering the best.

Actually,

doing the work gets you there faster than the
very
best
intentions.

There is a time and a place for everything.

You will not miss it.

When you embrace quality over quantity
and longevity over speed,
you will finally have space to breathe.

The good sometimes shouts louder
and looks shinier than the Great.

Take a step back and let the dust settle. Eventually you
will start to see the difference.

There is more magic in letting the process
take you to where you need to be,

than exhausting your existence rushing after
what was already yours.

Question everything.

Much of what we *think* we want has been created for our consumption and someone else's profit. Your welfare is not always in the equation…

…Maybe that is why even after you strain and stretch
to get what you *think* you want,

you stand squarely back at square one
wondering whether it was **worth it.**

Walking in purpose does not always require a frantic flurry of activity.

Spend time drawing mental, physical and spiritual boundaries that enlarge your capacity.

The goal is to walk my own path, more than I watch other people walk theirs.

Hold on to the vision, cling to your 'why' and let God reveal the 'how' each day.

The desperation to have things 'now' is what makes many of us give up too early.

Just as there is more to life than being born and dying,
there is more value in your life than
having a dream and finally realising it.

The in-between.

Seeing life as a series of events
coming together brick by brick,
instead of an hourglass that is running out
made me a <u>better builder.</u>

You are more than the current moment.
Your life is multi-dimensional.

Your worth does not change with title.

The best of life is reserved for those who turn inwards and uncover their true selves.

Fear calls everything a 'risk'
when in reality
sometimes it is called **obedience.**

It is called 'ground-breaking' for a reason.

Destruction comes before a rebirth and breaking new ground demands sweat. Be careful what you wish for.

Being called draws you in. It pulls you.

But stepping outside of your purpose requires that you do all the pushing.

Maybe that is why you are exhausted.

What if the people who finally 'made it' were the only ones with long-term commitment to the cause?

You can't outrun your calling.

The future belongs to those bold enough to respond to the life's call.

What is your response?

taking what I need
space for you to respond + journal your own thoughts:

IV

resilience

resilience

If the previous chapter was about (re)discovering who you are, this final section is its companion.

The beginning of something is always exciting. That is when we envision the future and daydream about overcoming potential hurdles with ease. These hurdles look a lot less threatening when they are a figment of your imagination. But when they materialise, they become more menacing than we ever anticipated. They evolve into immovable landmasses that threaten to derail our entire lives.

Sometimes the weight of these hurdles also brings darkness. Whether it is a new discovery made after a challenging therapy session, or a change of circumstance that shifts the landscape of your life, a shroud of darkness can follow in its wake. This darkness can look like insecurity, fear, depression, anxiety, lashing out and pushing people away.

These are the times that call for resilience: the ability to withstand pressure. Withstanding the pressure looks like resisting the temptation to panic or give up prematurely. Resisting is difficult by definition because it involves two opposing forces pressing against each other. And it can feel like the fight of your life.

Think of these parting words as your 'in case of emergency' kit, created to calm the panic and remind you that there is more to your story than the current pressures you face.

. . .

Have you ever considered that being 'in the thick of it'*
is beautiful in itself?

> 'the thick of it' /idiom/;
> being in the middle of the busiest,
> most intense part of a situation.

The pursuit of an easy life can drive us to great discomfort.

Comfort suffocates,
      challenge strengthens.

The sooner you realise that this is your life's work,
the calmer you will become.

A lifetime is a long time.

Hope is not always happy.

Sometimes it is a sober and silent internal posture.
It is the expectation that eventually, you will overcome.

Sometimes what you need more than anything is **space**.

Exchange the language of loneliness for an opportunity for greater intimacy with God.

Resistance is sometimes a signal to lean in and press on.

The 'perfect storm' sounds romantic when it is not you.

It is painful right now, and becomes perfect when you reach the other side.

A focused mind is never permanently deterred by disappointment.

Creating for the crowd is like feeding a beast that is never satisfied.

Fear tells you to run into the fire,
to keep firefighting at all costs.

Stillness gives you the space to strategize
and find the best solution.

Seek, be still and be expectant.

Create space in your life for God to step in.

Experiments do not always work out.

But they always provide the best lessons, and some of the best lessons make the most memorable stories.

Recycling.

Your world gets tighter when you focus on what is
missing,

leaving no room
for growth.

A generous heart rarely feels cheated, because it does not scramble for scraps.

There is a difference between being challenged
and living in strife.

Challenges bring out our bravest self,
strife exhausts our best.

The things that made you feel like a misfit can become your greatest asset.

Everything becomes beautiful in its own time.

Opposition is sometimes an opportunity
to stand by what you have established.

Your mission is too valuable to retreat.

The consolation we get for our mistakes is who we become on the other side.

The inability to clearly articulate what we need keeps us suspended in life's grey areas.

On feeling trapped.

The sooner we recognise that what is popular is not the same as what we need, the better.

The most you can ask of yourself is to do the best with what you have been given.

Prayer uproots worry.

taking what I need

space for you to respond + journal your own thoughts:

end.
thank you for reading.

Continue the *Take What You Need* journey

There is so much we can learn from each other, so we have established takingwhatineed.com: a collection of life lessons from you, the community.

Here you will be able to read wisdom and words of encouragement shared by other readers and submit your own.

Thank you for being a part of the TWYN community.

About the Author

Abiola Babarinde is a writer, speaker and communications strategist based in London, UK. Her work attempts to challenge life as we know it and uncover the things that matter most – the things we cannot see.

For more of her work, join The Inner Circle:
www.abiola.me

62547889R00066

Made in the USA
Middletown, DE
23 August 2019